GULLS...GULLS...GULLS...

BY GAIL GIBBONS

HOLIDAY HOUSE
NEW YORK

To GLENDA KRUEGER

Special thanks to Stephen Kress,
research biologist for the National Audubon Society.

Copyright © 1997 by Gail Gibbons
ALL RIGHTS RESERVED
Printed in the United States of America

Library of Congress Cataloging-in-Publication Data
Gibbons, Gail.
    Gulls—gulls—gulls / by Gail Gibbons. — 1st ed.
        p.   cm.
    Summary: Describes the life cycle, behavior patterns, and habitat
of various species of gulls, focusing on those found in North
America.
    ISBN 0-8234-1323-3
    1. Gulls—North America—Juvenile literature.   [1. Gulls.]
I. Title.
QL696.C46G53   1997   97-1266   CIP   AC
598.3'38—dc21

    ISBN 0-8234-1664-x (pbk.)

GULL

Gulls are among the most common birds seen along seashores. We see them feeding on sandy beaches, following fishing boats, and perching on rooftops in perfectly straight lines.

LARIDAE

Gulls are seen bobbing up and down on waves and soaring through the sky. They are members of the bird family called Laridae. There are forty-three different kinds of gulls in the world. They share many of the same characteristics.

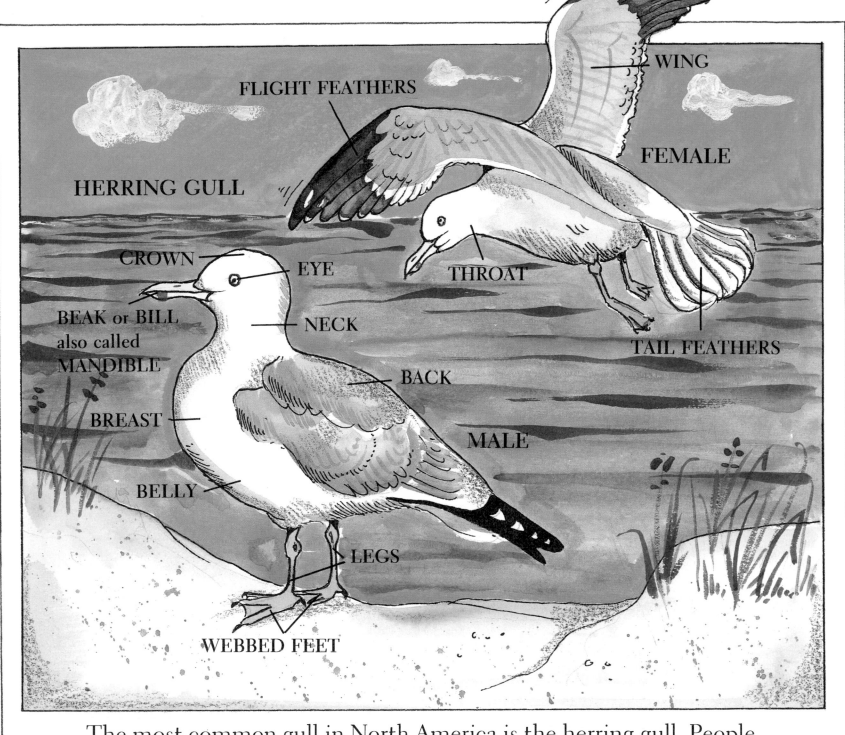

The most common gull in North America is the herring gull. People often call them sea gulls. It is about two feet (60 cm) long and has sleek, beautiful white-and-gray feathers with black wing tips. It has a wing spread of about four and one-half feet (135 cm). The male is usually a little bit bigger than the female.

Herring gulls have strong legs and webbed feet that make it easy for them to run around on land. Their ability to paddle through water makes them good swimmers.

UPDRAFT

These gulls are excellent fliers, too. Their long, narrow wings are perfect for soaring on updrafts of air and for gliding. They can soar and glide for long periods of time.

OIL GLAND

PREENING

A herring gull spends a lot of time taking care of its feathers, often two to three hours a day. This is called preening. An oil gland is located above the base of its tail. The bird presses out some oil with its beak and spreads the oil onto its feathers. This keeps the feathers waterproof and well-groomed.

MOLT means to lose feathers that are replaced by new ones.

Herring gulls, like other birds, molt. In the springtime they only molt some of their body feathers. In the fall they molt some of their body, wing and tail feathers.

HERRING GULL MIGRATION IN NORTH AMERICA

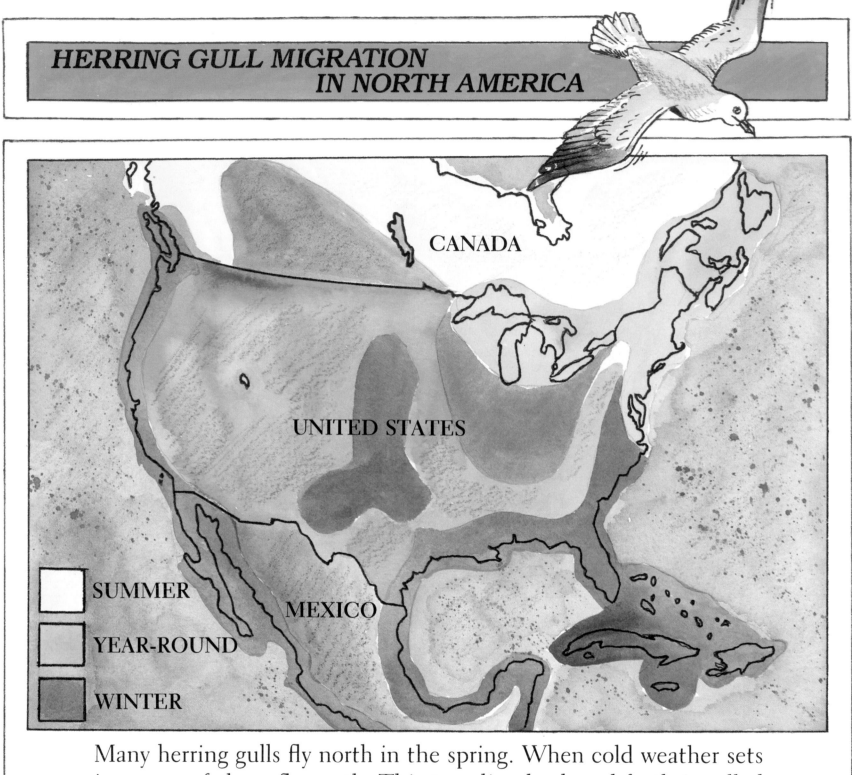

CANADA

UNITED STATES

MEXICO

SUMMER

YEAR-ROUND

WINTER

Many herring gulls fly north in the spring. When cold weather sets in, many of them fly south. This traveling back and forth is called migration. Herring gulls are found in groups called flocks along coastlines, lakes, rivers, and sometimes miles away from water.

Herring gulls eat almost anything. They even eat garbage at dumps. That's why they are called scavengers. They may eat blueberries; or follow plows across farm fields, snapping up uncovered worms and bugs; or follow fishing boats, scooping up leftovers from the day's catch. They also eat seafood such as sea urchins, clams, mussels, and small fish. Sometimes, they will drop a sea urchin or clam from high up onto a hard surface to break it open.

COURTING

ANGER

TERRITORY

Herring gulls communicate in many ways. They bob their heads up and down, and peck at the ground while courting. A gull stretching forward and pointing its beak is showing anger. Grass-pulling by a male herring gull means, "This is my area."

They also use different sounds to communicate with each other. Often, they can be heard screeching and wailing. Scientists are not certain what many of these sounds mean.

When herring gulls settle down to rest or sleep they are "roosting." Often, when they are roosting, they fly off to their favorite place on land or float on water.

Herring gulls sleep for short periods of time. Mostly, they sleep with their heads resting on their backs.

During the winter months, light brown streaks appear on their heads.

COLONY

When spring comes, it is breeding time. Most herring gulls return to where they were hatched, often to rugged isolated islands. They come together with other nesting gulls to form a colony. Sometimes they use the same nesting site season after season.

Usually the same pair mates again and raises its young together. The males and females look very much alike, but the herring gulls seem to have no trouble recognizing their partners.

While courting, they chase each other playfully. Sometimes, they face each other and bob their heads up and down, and pcck at the ground. Other times they jerk their bills up and down.

NEST

It is nest-building time. The male and female scrape an area with their feet, usually a grassy area on the ground. They gather grasses, mosses and dried weeds, and place them on the nesting area. Slowly a snug, round nest appears.

Soon after their nest is built, the female lays tan eggs with brown splotches. Female gulls usually lay one to four eggs. Both parents take turns keeping the eggs warm, incubating them. While one gull is busy sitting on the eggs, the other one searches for food and guards the area from intruders.

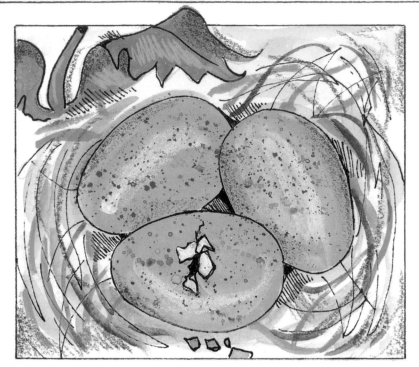

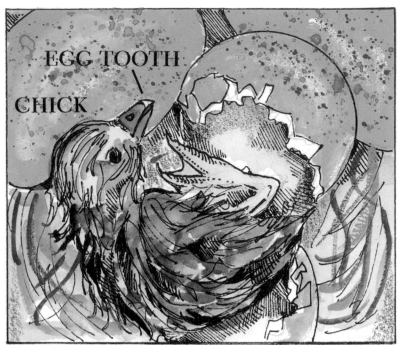

EGG TOOTH

CHICK

After about one month, an egg begins to crack. A herring gull chick pecks its way out of the shell with its egg tooth. The nesting parent looks down at the wet, sticky chick and once again gently nestles down.

When all the chicks have hatched, brooding time begins. The parents start feeding and caring for their chicks. The chicks learn to find the food the parents bring to them by pecking at the red mark on their parents' beaks. Then the parents take turns regurgitating, or throwing up, their partially digested food for the chicks to eat.

The chicks grow. Their fluffy down feathers have dark tan spots. The parents continue to feed them and keep them safe. The chicks cuddle and play. They practice flying by fluttering up and down.

FLEDGLING

When the chicks are about five weeks old, they are called fledglings and are almost as big as their parents. Their feathers are mostly brown and gray. It is time to leave the nest. Soon the young gulls are able to fly away and live on their own. In about four years they will have their adult feathers and will return to make their own nesting areas and raise their young.

About one hundred years ago there were few gulls in the United States. They were hunted for their feathers, which were used for decorating hats and other things. Today we see many gulls because they are protected by laws.

Scientists have learned that all gulls play an important part in the balance of our natural world. For example, they are scavengers and help keep our seashores and other places clean.

Gulls are beautiful birds to watch soar through the skies. Their cries
are mysterious and haunting.

It is fun to watch gulls exploring their world.

WHERE SOME COMMON GULLS ARE FOUND

HERRING GULL

North America

LAUGHING GULL

Seacoasts of the
Atlantic and the
Gulf of Mexico

FRANKLIN'S GULL

North Central United
States and Central Canada

WESTERN GULL

Pacific seacoast

BONAPARTE'S GULL

North America

RING-BILLED GULL

North America

CALIFORNIA GULL

Western United States
and Western Canada

GREAT BLACK-BACKED GULL

Atlantic seacoast

GULLS...GULLS...GULLS...

Gulls can drink both fresh water and salt water.

Some gull colonies have thousands of nesting gulls.

Gulls can live to be thirty years old.

The smallest gull, the little gull, is only eleven inches (28 cm) long. It is found along the Northeastern seacoast of the United States and around the Great Lakes.

The largest gull is the great black-backed gull. It is about two and one-half feet (75 cm) long, with a wing spread of about six feet (180 cm).

Sometimes people from the National Audubon Society or the Fish and Wildlife Service put numbered bands on the gulls' legs to track the birds' movements.

Often scientists and bird-watchers spend time hidden in structures called blinds from where they can study gulls. That way they don't disturb the birds.

In Salt Lake City, Utah, there is a bronze statue of two California gulls. This is to honor the gulls that saved farm crops from destruction by grasshoppers in 1848.

The ivory gull, which nests in the high Arctic of North America, is the only gull that is pure white year round.

The laughing gull gets its name from its loud, laughing-like cry.

Terns are related to gulls. They are smaller and have a deeply forked tail.

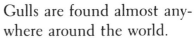

Gulls are found almost anywhere around the world.

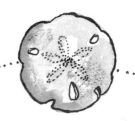